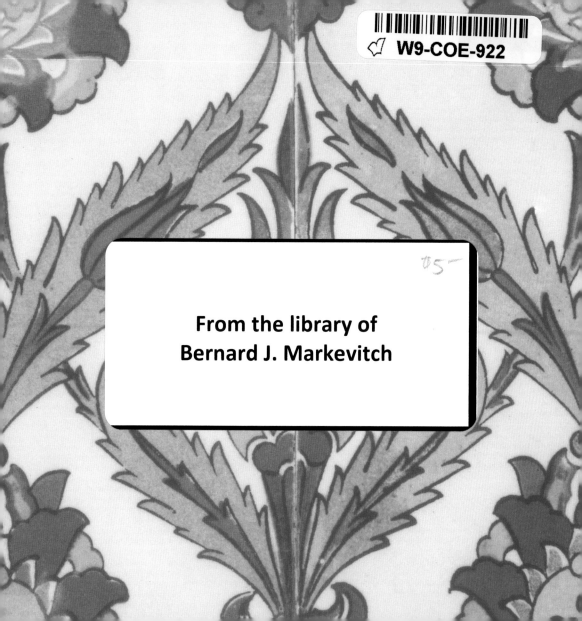

Tulips

Emelie Tolley and Chris Mead

Published by Clarkson Potter/Publishers, 201 East 50th Street, New York, New York 10022.
Member of the Crown Publishing Group.

Random House, Inc. New York, Toronto, London, Sydney, Auckland

CLARKSON N. POTTER, POTTER, and colophon are trademarks of Clarkson N. Potter, Inc.

Printed in China

Design by Margaret Hinders

Library of Congress Cataloging-in-Publiscation Data
Tolley, Emelie.
Tulips/Emelie Tolley and Chris Mead.
1.Tulips. I Mead, Chris. Title.
SB413.T9T655 1998
635.9'3432—dc21   97-20915
CIP
ISBN 0-609-60132-6
10 9 8 7 6 5 4 3 2 1
First Edition

To Terry

—C.M.

To Alex and Alexander—for being there

—E.T.

Acknowledgments

To all those who helped us gather tulip memorabilia and information, we say thank you, but especially to Peter Tarantino, Matthew Mead, Michael Mead, Beryl Ratcliff, Alexander Jakowec, Alex Sigmon, Berns Frye, Kara Fogarty, Albert Morris, Kathleen Scupp, Donald Norton, John and Sandy Horvitz, James Cramer and Dean Johnson, Robin Strashun, Paul Winsor, Kim Polley, Pam Huber, Anne and Susan Madonia. D. J. White, Howard and Linda Stein, Rebecca Cole, Tonk van Lexmond and Emy ten Seldoam of Terra Publishing Co., The Netherlands Board of Tourism, Jeroen van Seeters and the International Flower Bulb Center, the National Museum of Het Loo Palace, Kees Noordermeer, Mrs. T. Bader-Heemskerk, the Frans Hals Museum, Mahmet Yazzan, Siska Osman, and Anne Vandervord. As always, we are grateful to all our friends at Clarkson Potter who translate our work into a book, especially Maggie Hinders for her sensitive handling of the text and photographs, Margot Schupf for keeping things on track, and, above all, Pam Krauss, our editor, for her constant support, encouragement, and patience.

Introduction

L ike the first robin, tulips signal the arrival of spring, their gay blossoms a welcome sight after the drabness of winter. No flower in history has captured our imaginations—and wallets—quite so fully. In the seventeenth century, tulip mania raged through Holland; making and breaking millionaires through the furious trading of bulbs. The same obsession on a lesser scale gripped the Turks, engulfed the French and even seduced the reserved English.

The mania may have ceased, but the tulip's popularity continues, with millions of bulbs cultivated in Holland, Britain, France, the United States, Australia, and Japan each year. Originally cherished as a symbol of luxury, as well as for its exotic beauty, the tulip's amazing variety of colors and shapes continues to bewitch gardeners and artisans. Feathered, fringed, and streaked, they appear in every hue: only blue and pure black have managed to elude the breeders of bulbs. Tulip fanciers can choose from more than 3,000 named varieties in shapes ranging from the delicate lily tulip to the flamboyant parrot or the more subtle botanicals. Over the years tulips have been celebrated in paintings and prints; ceramics; textiles; metalwork; and architectural ornament. They have enhanced the beauty of gardens, carried a message of love, and even brought pleasure to the gourmand. So plant some tulips in your garden or buy a generous bunch from the florist, and enjoy their beauty as kings and commoners have through the centuries.

A General History

Carolus Clusius
(1526-1609)

Tulips, small, sturdy, and quite unlike those we know today, grew wild in the mountains and fields of central Asia centuries ago. Though they figure prominently in the arts of that continent, they didn't reach Europe until the latter half of the sixteenth century. It's thought they arrived in 1554 through the auspices of Ogier Ghiselin de Busbecq, the Viennese ambassador to the Ottoman court of Sultan Suleyman the Magnificent, who sent some bulbs to Emperor Ferdinand I of Austria, then later carried seed home with him. Although known to the natives as *lalé*, de Busbecq called the bulbs *tulipan*, no doubt misunderstanding a translator comparing the shape of the flower to a Turkish turban.

Some of de Busbecq's plants were given to Carolus Clusius (botanist Charles de l'Ecluse), head of the Imperial Gardens of Vienna. When religious disputes led him to resettle in Holland as the curator of the Hortus Botanical Gardens at Leiden, he cultivated the bulbs, but sold them for such outrageous prices that thieves stole them and spread the bounty. This was the birth of the Dutch tulip industry.

Tulips soon became popular among the gentry of Austria, Germany, Flanders, the Lowlands, and France spurring the cultivation of new varieties and sending prices skyrocketing. In France a feverish desire to own tulip bulbs erupted in the early part of the seventeenth century, causing a miller to sell his mill for one rare bulb called 'Mere Brune'; and a groom delightedly accepted a

single bulb of 'Marriage de ma Fille' as his bride's entire dowry. Women even eschewed jewelry in favor of tucking tulip flowers into the low-cut bodices of their gowns.

The tulip arrived in England in 1577–78 and was well established by the early seventeenth century, when John Parkinson described 140 varieties commonly seen in English gardens, including the 50 different varieties growing in the royal gardens. They remained favorites of the English aristocracy until the mid-eighteenth century.

When Dutch and English settlers set sail for North America, they took tulip bulbs with them and sent for more. In the early 1800s a colony of Dutch settlers founded the town of Holland, Michigan, now one of the major bulb-growing areas in the United States. Thomas Jefferson planted tulips at Monticello, and they were popular enough for a Boston nursery to offer fifty varieties in 1860. Many formal gardens still have tulip beds based on eighteenth- and nineteenth-century plans. More recently, the Northwest has become a major growing area, hosting a tulip festival each spring.

The English also planted tulips in Australia, re-creating their beloved English gardens wherever the climate permitted. And when Canada gave refuge to the Dutch royal family during World War II, Queen Juliana's thank-you gift of 100,000 bulbs began an ongoing custom of tulip displays in most major Canadian cities.

Even Japan is not immune to the tulip's seductive beauty. Dutch merchants began trading bulbs there in the nineteenth century, and bulb growing is now a major business: 120 million bulbs are planted each year, often as an alternative crop to rice.

Indeed, the pretty little flowers that once grew wild in central Asia have spread their magic far and wide, casting a spell on all who appreciate their beauty and gay color.

Birthday Greeting

The Emerald success in love,
The Tulip self reliance;
Thy radiant star up in the sky
Foretells courage and defiance.

Bloembollenvelden

Bloembollen

Tulipomania

Although the first shipment of tulip bulbs arrived in Antwerp in 1562, Tulipomania didn't start until many years later and reached its height in 1634–37. As seeds and bulbs proliferated throughout Holland, anyone with a spot to grow even a few flowers became a potential grower—and a possible millionaire. Each carried the hope that a spontaneous trick of nature might cause his bulb to produce an especially desirable new variety, a mutation that we now know was caused by a virus transmitted by aphids.

By the mid-seventeenth century the Dutch had at least several hundred varieties of tulips on record, and people from all walks of life were caught up in the frenzy of trading. Junk dealers, chimney sweeps, and maidservants, as well as poets and painters, became players in the game, their greed encouraging them to ignore common sense as prices escalated far beyond the real value of the bulbs.

Rumors of overnight fortunes were spread quickly, fueling the mania. A ritual of trading was quickly established, and clubs known as *collegiums* met at a semisecret network of inns and taverns throughout the country. Although outside stock market regulations, the traders devised their

own elaborate set of rules. As the madness increased, saner souls looked askance at what was transpiring. Jan Brueghel II satirized the dealings in a painting depicting monkeys buying and selling tulips over the sort of lavish meal that was traditionally part of the transaction. As prices soared even children were pressed into service and sent to the trading clubs as spies. Growers guarded the bulbs in their gardens with ingenious systems of alarm bells that warned of unexpected visitors.

Eventually bulbs were sold in name only, turning over ten times in one day making a profit for everyone with nary a bulb in sight. Not surprisingly, fraud was rampant. The mad trading caused prices to rise and rise. In the most famous sale of all, one Viceroy bulb was exchanged for two loads of wheat, four loads of rye, four fat oxen, eight fat pigs, twelve sheep, two barrels of butter, a thousand pounds of cheese, two hogsheads of wine, four barrels of special beer, a silver beaker, a suit of clothes, and a complete bed, the whole being valued at 2,500 florins. Workers traded their tools for bulbs, and deals were augmented by horses, carriages, even houses.

The mania started to subside at the end of 1636, when the supply of bulbs became greater than the demand. By January 1637 prices began to drop sharply, and panic ensued as people tried desperately to cut their losses.

A series of resolutions issued by everyone from the florist's guild up to Parliament put an end to the madness, and by April 1637 the maximum price of a tulip bulb was set at 50 florins, leaving many tulips like the revered Semper Augustus worth just 1/100 of their previous value. Although an exact estimate of the havoc wrought by the mania is impossible to determine, it is known that tens of thousands of people were ruined. Careers and reputations were destroyed and entire families were doomed to poverty, all because of the lovely tulip.

Bonne Fête

The Turkish Tulip

Turkish society as a whole has always been enamored of flowers, never considering them a strictly feminine interest. So it's not surprising that when the tulip reached Turkey in the mid-fifteenth century, the delicate almond-shaped flower whose long pointed petals resemble today's *Tulipa acuminata* became a Turkish favorite. Mehmet II, the conqueror of Constantinople and builder of the Topkapi Palace, was a keen gardener; while Europeans were still content with simple herb gardens and orchards, he had ornamental gardens abloom with tulips.

The ruling House of Osman adopted the shapely tulip as a symbol of royalty. Its alluring colors and shapes made it a favored motif in both textiles and the beautiful tiles and pottery from Isnik. As the Ottoman Empire reached it's cultural apex under the rule of Suleyman the Magnificent in the sixteenth century, the obsession with tulips continued. The era was known as the Tulip Age, and as in Holland, people from all walks of life bought bulbs. The tulip's reign ended only when Mohammed IV declared the ranunculus "more alluring."

Ahmed III revived interest in the tulip in the early eighteenth century, spurring a tulip cult that handsomely rewarded poets who sang its praises and growers who produced new varieties. This obsessive love of tulips threatened to escalate into a mania of the sort that had gripped Holland, prompting the sultan to exhort the mayor to control prices.

Nonetheless, the sultan's palace gardens were filled with no fewer than half a million bulbs, and records created by Sheikh Mohammed Lalézaré (The Tulip Chief) listed over 1,300 varieties. Tulip fetes became the rage of the Turkish court. From the description of one such celebration written in April 1726, they were truly magical events that continued nightly

so long as the tulips remained in flower.

Under Ahmed's successor, Mahmud I, less elaborate tulip shows were staged in the courtyards of the Seraglio to celebrate important domestic events. An amphitheater of wooden stands with shelves along both sides held vases of cut tulips. Lamps, glass globes filled with various colored waters, and cages of canaries were placed among them. More flowers were fashioned into pyramids, towers, or archways or spread on the ground in patterns resembling a carpet. Then at sunset, the outer gates of the courtyard were closed, a cannon fired, and the harem doors opened, releasing the women of the harem cavorting among eunuchs bearing 1,000 fragrant torches. Filled with excitement at the glorious sight and a night of freedom, they paraded about, their sole aim to attract the attention of their master for the evening.

Today these fantasies are echoed, though on a far less glorious scale, by the Tulipfestival held in the town of Emirgan, on the Bosphorous near Istanbul.

A Multitude of Tulips

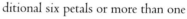

T ulips, a member of the Liliaceae family, grow from a bulb that sends forth a gaily colored flower on a strong, straight stem. Once found growing wild in the mountains of Asia, tulips have been so widely hybridized that the species, hybrids, and cultivars now number into the thousands, including some with eight rather than the traditional six petals or more than one flower per stem. Tulips were originally classified as early, mid-season, or late flowering varieties according to their bloom time. With the proliferation of flowers developed by growers and occurring spontaneously in the field through sports (or mutated bulblets), a more precise system imposed order on the tulip world in 1913, resulting in more definitive classifications.

Fashion always plays an enormous part in a particular tulip's popularity and, consequently, in the classifications. Broken tulips with their flamboyant colors and markings were the darlings of growers in the first half of the nineteenth century. A gardening book from later in the century saves its praise for the late-flowering single, with its strong stem and large cup-shaped flower, while dismissing the lovely peony-shaped tulip as too showy. When the Darwin hybrid came along in the early 1900s, self-colored tulips suddenly became fashionable; varieties proliferated dramatically.

Currently all tulips are divided into fifteen divisions:

Single early tulips Seldom more than 15 inches in height, they often have a pleasing scent. Among them are two of the oldest known tulips: 'Silver Standard' dating from 1637, and the red and yellow 'Keizerskroon', which has been around since 1750.

Early doubles About 10 inches tall, they come in all colors, but are not as robust as late doubles. 'Murillo', dating from 1860, is one of the best known and has produced 101 sports.

Darwin hybrids A cross between the Darwin tulip and *T. fosteriana*, these tall, stately, mid-season bloomers are robust and naturalize well. This most widely cultivated tulip has the familiar egg shape with a slightly squarer bottom.

*indicates bulbs suitable for forcing

Triumphs This mid-season bloomer with strong flowers in an extraordinary range of color, was introduced following World War I. Though smaller, they are almost as popular as Darwin hybrids.

Single late tulips Encompass the old Darwins, cottage tulips, and the Dutch and English breeder tulips, some of which reach 40 inches in height and include interesting color combinations. Several tulips date from 1630: 'Gala Beauty', a yellow and carmine flamed flower, and 'Zomerschoon', whose salmon on cream flower is rare and expensive.

Double late or peony-flowered tulips Earlier varieties had weak stems and hanging heads, problems that have been overcome with the strong, new cultivars.

Rembrandt tulips (broken tulips) Primarily of historic interest, the Rembrandt's tendency to harbor thetulip-breaking virus has made them virtually obsolete commercially.

Lily-flowered tulips Valued most for their beautiful shape. Once part of the cottage tulip classification, they became a separate class in 1958.

Fringed tulips Once grouped with the cottage and Darwin classifications because they were relatively rare, these delicately fringed blooms became a separate classification in 1981.

'Viridiflora' tulips Admired for their interesting touch of green. In cultivation since 1700, they have never been seen in the wild. They received their own classification in 1981.

Parrot tulips Known for over three centuries, though little is known of their origin. These flamboyant ruffled and fringed flowers cannot be reproduced from seed: they all develop from sports. Several tulips from 1665—

'Admiral de Constantinople' and lutea major—and 'Perfecta Markgraaf' from 1750 are still available.

The remaining four classes are botanical tulips, those most closely related to flowers found in the wild. They bloom early, sometimes even making an appearance during a mild January or February. Though smaller and less showy than horticultural tulips, they are more robust, growing from zone 3 south to zone 8. These true perennials naturalize well, particularly in rock gardens. Many have

three to seven flowers per stem, often with contrasting markings. A few have ornamental foliage. The three with their own classification are *T. kaufmanniana*, *T. fosteriana* and. *T. gregeii*

The *Tulipa*, or species tulips, are those cultivated from the wild. Though most are small, a few produce giant flowers; some are multiflowered.

Tulips in the Garden

Growing tulips is an easy task. Although seeds take up to seven years to flower, bulbs are planted in fall and, assuming they escape the ravenous appetites of burrowing rodents, will burst forth in glorious bloom the following spring. When buying bulbs, look for firm specimens with no black spots or growth, mold, bruises, or cuts, then plant them as soon as possible or keep them in a spot where the temperature never goes above 70° F. to ensure the largest flowers. Since tulips prefer a light sandy soil, many gardeners recommend planting them on a thin layer of sand or mixing sand with the soil in the planting hole. If your soil is heavy, dig in some compost, fine

gravel, or grit before planting to help improve the drainage and add a little bulb booster to supply nutrients.

Bulbs can be planted, pointed end up, anytime from October to the end of November. Plant horticultural varieties 6 to 8 inches deep, botanical varieties 2 to 4 inches deep; and allow 3 to 5 inches between bulbs. Plant bulbs in an irregular pattern for a more natural look or in clumps for a stunning display. In cool areas, protect newly planted bulbs with mulch, then remove the mulch in the spring as soon as new growth starts. In warm areas, condition the bulbs in the refrigerator for eight to ten weeks before planting to trick them into resting and to encourage long stems. (Remove any fruit from the refrigerator first, since it gives off ethylene gas, which can inhibit bloom.)

Water after planting in the fall, and once a week in the spring in unseasonably dry weather. Consider setting the bulbs under deciduous trees. Although sun helps develop color, one hot day can shorten the life of your flowers.

To foil the animals who consider bulbs a delicacy, plant them in wire-mesh baskets and feed with commercial bulb booster instead of the more traditional and tastier bone meal. To banish tulip-hungry rabbits in the spring, spray the green leaves with a mixture of cayenne pepper and water.

Once your tulips have finished blooming, cut the stems to prevent the plants from setting seed, which depleats their energy. Leave the foliage intact until it yellows, this helps the bulb store energy. Then dig up the bulbs, clean and dry them, and store them in paper bags in a dark cool place until it's time to plant again the following fall.

While digging and storing is the traditional method of growing tulips, especially in formal beds, some varieties can be left in the ground to rebloom the following year. Botanical tulips, which bloom in March or April, naturalize readily. Close to the wild varieties, they include *Tulipa fosteriana, T. clusiana, T. pulchella, T. praestans, T. sylvestris, T. violacea, T. greigii, T. turkestanica, T. saxatilis,* and *T. Sprengeri.* They're suitable for growing in zones 3 through 8, are disease resistant, and thrive in full sun or light shade. Darwin hybrids, especially those marked "for naturalizing," will also bloom for up to five years if planted several inches deeper than usual and nourished with a little low-nitrogen bulb food in the fall and spring.

Since tulips like very cold weather, they survive without digging better in colder climes than in warm, where they are best treated as an annual. However, over time any tulip will finally wear out and need replacing. As the tulips get weaker, consider transplanting them to the cutting garden where the smaller blossoms can be gathered for bouquets. If overcrowding lessens the bloom, simply dig the bulbs up after the foliage has died down. Pull the small bulblets off, then replant both large and small, temporarily relegating the bulblets, which won't bloom until the second year, to an obscure spot.

The Potted Tulip

Nothing brightens gray winter days like a pot of colorful tulips, so pot enough to see you through the dreary season. Catalogs and garden centers indicate which of their offerings are best for forcing. Plant the bulbs close together in a pot with good drainage. Three bulbs fit nicely into a 5-inch pot; six to eight can be arranged in a 6-inch pot. Use regular potting soil; set the bulbs so the tip is just above the surface of the soil, water thoroughly.

Remember that even tulips for indoor forcing must experience at least 10 weeks of cold in order to bloom, so place the potted bulbs in the refrigerator or dig the pots into the ground and let nature provide the cold. Select a cool, shaded area and dig a trench deep enough for the pots and a cover of mulch 3 to 4 inches deep. This protects them against freezing and allows easy removal even when the ground is frozen.

Any time after mid-December, start bringing the potted tulips in at two-week intervals for an on-going parade of blooms. Once the bulbs are inside, keep them in a dark, coolish place (about 65° F.) and water regularly. When the foliage is 1 or 2 inches high, place the pots in the sun. In a few weeks you will be rewarded with a colorful display. Once the blossoms have faded, throw the bulbs away: forcing will have depleted their energy.

Fanciful Tulip Tales

I t is rumored that tulips are a favorite flower of fairies. An English tale tells of the old Devonshire woman who year after year grew beautiful beds of tulips. All spring she tended them carefully, and when they finally burst into bloom, she heard sweet strains of music floating up to her window at midnight as their colorful bells swayed in time to the melody. This always brought a smile, for she knew the pixies from the nearby wood were singing and rocking their tiny babies to sleep in the roomy cups. For the entire month they bloomed, the woman never allowed anyone to pick the blossoms. Alas, when the woman died, her practical-minded son plowed up the tulips and planted parsnips in their stead. The angry pixies breathed on the earth and from then on the son was never able to grow anything in the garden. But the pixies remembered the kind old woman, and although no one cared for her grave, instead of weeds beautiful flowers sprang from the earth every day and at midnight soft music floated through the air.

The elusive black tulip is the star of another story. When word that a cobbler at The Hague had succeeded in cultivating a black tulip reached some Haarlem florists, they immediately offered to buy the bulb for 1,500 florins. The cobbler agreed, but as soon as he put the bulb in their hands, the florists threw it to the ground and trampled it, explaining that they, too, had a black tulip and wanted no competition. Indeed, they confessed that they would willingly have paid 10,000 florins. Inconsolable, the cobbler took to his bed and soon after died of disappointment. To this day the only true black tulip is in Alexandre Dumas's famous story *La Tulipe Noire*.

A Bouquet of Tulips

A lush bouquet of tulips is a cheery sight at any time of the year. Garden tulips will last longer if cut in the early morning while still partially closed. Even better, catch the flowers while they are still in bud but with at least one-half to two-thirds of the bud showing color. Cut too green, they won't mature. At the florist's, select partially closed flowers with fresh green leaves and firm petals.

To condition cut tulips for longest life, recut the stems at an angle, removing the lower white solid section, then plunge the blooms into cool water up to their necks and set them in a cool place for a few hours—or overnight, if possible. If at any point the stems seem a bit droopy, wrap the tulips snugly in some wet newspaper and place them in warm water for a few hours.

Use a chicken-wire frog rather than oasis as a foundation for your arrangement: it allows the thirsty tulips to drink more easily. Either arrange the tulips tightly so they help support each other or give them room to take on the gracefully curving stems that come naturally, but always put the most open blooms in the center of the bouquet. *Never mix in newly cut daffodils: their sap is deadly to tulips.* As you work, remember that the tulips will lean toward the strongest source of light and the flowers will open wide and the stems appear to lengthen as they age. Add flower preservative to the water and don't forget to keep refilling the vase: tulips drink copiously throughout the five to eight days they last. Every three days, recut the stems and replace the preservative solution. An occasional misting is also beneficial.

THE TULIP PRESERVED

🌷 🌷 🌷 🌷

Tulips dried in silica gel retain all their charm. An important part of period arrangements ever since Thomas Jefferson used their graceful blooms in the arrangements at Monticello, preserved tulips are just as appealing in a simple bouquet. Petals that fall from fresh bouquets will air dry, retaining their color, and make lovely additions to potpourris.

Materials

Fresh tulips
Silica gel
Airtight box
Florist's wire
Green florist's tape (optional)

1. Cut the stem 1¼-inch below the stem.
2. In the airtight box, make a 1¼-inch-deep layer of silica gel. Set the tulip cups gently into the silica gel, burying the stem and leaving 1¼ inches between the sides of the box and between flowers. Carefully spoon more silica gel around the outsides of the flowers to support them, then gently pour more over them to a depth of 1¼ inches. Cover the box and set aside until the flowers are completely dry, 3–4 days.
3. When the flowers are dry, remove them with care and shake off any excess silica gel. Carefully insert a piece of florist's wire through the stem and up through the flower. Make a little hook at the end, then gently pull the wire back through the stem until the hook catches in the flower. Wrap the wire with green florist's tape.

For brilliant plants to
charm the eye
What plant can with
the Tulip vie?
—ANONYMOUS

The Decorative Tulip

T he simple, graphic shape and graceful lines of a tulip, as well as its cheerful associations, have made it a favored motif among centuries of artists and craftspeople. Their glowing colors and varied shapes have adorned tiles and stained glass, table linens and tapestries, gilded leather, silver teapots and pottery plates, sconces and chandeliers, paintings, and elaborately crafted or simple painted furniture. Even Chinese porcelain exported during Tulipomania had tulips incorporated into the design. And though neither vases nor bouquets were common in seventeenth-century houses,

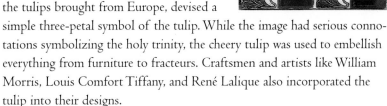

tulipières, or tulip vases with holes or spouts on all sides, each of which held a single tulip, were created so the rare blossoms could be shown to best advantage.

The Pennsylvania Dutch, inspired by the tulips brought from Europe, devised a simple three-petal symbol of the tulip. While the image had serious connotations symbolizing the holy trinity, the cheery tulip was used to embellish everything from furniture to fracteurs. Craftsmen and artists like William Morris, Louis Comfort Tiffany, and René Lalique also incorporated the tulip into their designs.

After the Depression the tulip became a popular motif, adding a note of cheer to yellowware bowls, kitchen canisters, supermarket glasses, children's toys, garden decorations, and more. Today they continue to bloom on dress fabrics, curtains, quilts, and wallpaper and blossom year-round in bouquets crafted from metal, silk, paper, wood, and even beads.

THE STENCILED TULIP

You can find stylized tulip designs to adapt for a stencil on items as diverse as tablecloths and dish towels, tiles, posters, and kitchen cannisters. You can use the motif as here on place mats, as well as on curtains, kitchen cabinets, trays, or furniture. The finished mats measure 12" × 18".

Materials for 4 place mats

4 pieces of heavy cotton, 13" × 19"
Tracing paper (optional)
Graphite pencil
Oiled stencil card
Masking tape
Craft knife
Red fabric paint
Green fabric paint
Stencil brush
White thread

1. Prewash the fabric to remove any sizing. Iron.
2. Select a design and have it photocopied or trace it. Cut it apart if necessary to rework it into a rectangular shape, then use a copier to rescale your design to fit the placemat.
3. Use a soft pencil to cover the back of the design completely. Attach the design to the oiled card with masking tape and

go over the design with a pencil to transfer it to the card. If the pattern is complex, it may be easier to work with several different stencils. A border, for example, can be executed by repeating a partial stencil, or different colors can be done on different stencils. Carefully cut out the design with the craft knife. If you are using more than one stencil, notch the cards so the design can be kept in register as you apply it.

4. Affix the fabric to a hard surface with masking tape, then affix the stencil to the fabric the same way. Dip the stencil brush into some of the red paint, then dab the brush on a piece of moist paper toweling to remove any excess. Carefully dab the brush over the red sections of the design, working slowly in a stroking or circular motion. Don't saturate the fabric with paint. Complete the green sections in the same manner.

5. Allow the mats to dry for at least one hour, then set the color by heating an iron to the "cotton" setting and smoothly pressing the mat. Let the iron remain on each section for at least 30 seconds. Hem the mats and attach trimming if desired.

Here tulips bloom as they are told.

—RUPERT BROOKE, BERLIN 1912

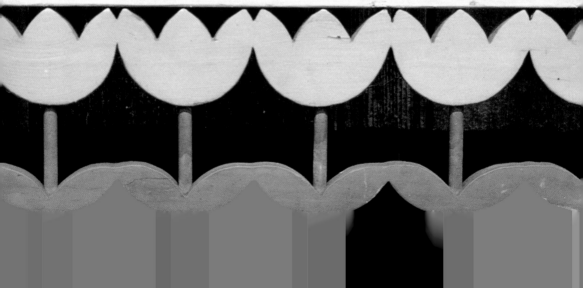

The Artful Tulip

T he earliest known drawing of a tulip was Conrad Gessner's 1561 rendering of a tulip seen in Vienna, and eight illustrations appear in an herbal from 1565. But likenesses of tulips proliferated during Tulipomania when Florilegia—collections of engravings compiled into books—were created both to catalog growers' stocks and as personal reference for connoisseurs. These Florilegia also became copy books for craftsmen.

Dutch flower paintings, rich, complicated, and the epitome of floral still lives, reputedly came into being when a lady who was too poor to buy a bouquet commissioned an artist to paint one for her as a substitute. Actually, bouquets as we know them today had little or no part in the domestic life of that time: these beguiling flower paintings were nothing more than ostentatious displays of the owner's wealth. Some depict bouquets fashioned from as many as six dozen different flowers, all of which bloomed at different times and could have been gathered together only in the artist's imagination. However, such famous artists as Ambrosius Dosschaert are known to have visited the Hortus Botanicas in Leyden to paint live tulips. Often the painting included such unlikely bits of nature as an ant, a fly, a cricket, a grasshopper, a moth, a lizard, or even a skull, none of which would have been found in a tidy household. Occasionally they were symbolic: the

artist might use a mouse to represent gluttony, while fallen leaves signified the ravages of time, and snails, slugs, beetles, and lizards helped remind the viewer that the beauty he was gazing on must fade and wither as does human life. But the items in the paintings also flaunted the owner's wealth: Ming vases, rare tulips like the 'Semper Augustus', expensive shells from faraway seas, Persian carpets, and precious stones all found their way into the artist's vision.

Many years later, tulips also showed up in American paintings as a symbol of the owner's wealth. A portrait done in 1765 by John Single-ton Copley of the twenty-eight-year-old wife of a prosperous Plymouth merchant testifies to the rarity and value of certain tulips in the colonies. In it, Elizabeth Watson holds a par-rot tulip, possibly the only example of its kind in the New England area, and thus worth far more than the painter's fee.

Since then many amateur painters have tried their talents at capturing the simple lines of the tulip in naive paintings. Postcards and stationery are adorned with its likeness and even advertisers have used its graphic appeal to promote their products.

HOLLAND
1948
JUBILEE YEAR

fipa diluté lutea,   obfcure aurantio colore imifto.   Tulipa alba coccineo fafciata.

Gelb mit dunckel   pomeranzen gelb   Weiße   mit Carmin roth geftreifte Tul

IN AN OLD DUTCH GARDEI
(BY AN OLD DUTCH MILL)

Lyric by
MACK GORDON

Music by
WILL GROSZ

Featured by
Everett
Hoagland
and his Orchestra

TULIP BRAND

APPLES

A Token of Love

L ike roses, tulips have long been associated with romance. The Persians saw them as a symbol of perfect love and created a language of flowers based on their various hues: red tulips were a declaration of love; yellow meant hopeless love; variegated blossoms conveyed that the recipient had beautiful eyes; while a black center symbolized a heart burnt by love.

Although Parkinson questioned the tulip's aphrodisiacal qualities in his famous herbal, the Turks used them in love potions. And through the years, lovers have played on its name, accompanying bouquets of tulips with a message expressing the hope that "our two lips will soon meet again."

IT'S TULIP TIME
IN HOLLAND
TWO LIPS ARE CALLING ME

JEROME H. REMICK & CO.
NEW YORK   DETROIT

🌷 55 🌷

The Tasty Tulip

I t is said a Dutch merchant who once received a shipment of precious goods from the East spotted what appeared to be onions among the silks and velvets and ordered one prepared for his lunch, only to discover that he had consumed a bulb of the rare and expensive 'Semper Augustus' tulip. More believable, perhaps, is another version that had an English cloth merchant enjoying a similar repast and instructing his gardener to plant the remaining onions in the garden. When the flowers appeared in the spring, he was pleasantly surprised.

Foolish though these stories may be, when the tulip first arrived in Europe, the "foodies" of the day attempted without much success to turn ordinary bulbs into a delicacy. In 1597 the Englishman John Gerard said they "may be eaten, and are not unpleasant nor any way offensive meat, but rather good and nourishing." A German apothecary preserved tulip bulbs in sugar; the English dressed theirs with oil and vinegar. But it wasn't until the devastating food shortages in Holland during World War II that their nutritional value was truly appreciated.

The bulbs *can* be substituted for onions in most recipes, but while their texture is similar they are more expensive and less flavorful. Sliced and fried, tulip bulbs add an interesting crunch to

salads; while the stamens, washed, dried, and sautéed in butter, taste something like asparagus.

But it is the petals that cooks generally find most interesting in the kitchen, because even though they have little taste, their color enhances any dish. Chop a few and toss them into a salad; sugar them to decorate a cake; stuff them like grape leaves for a colorful appetizer; use them to scoop up dips; or try the recipes that follow.

COOL TULIPS

🌷 🌷 🌷 🌷

An ice bowl filled with brilliant tulips makes a spectacular serving dish. Equally useful for punch,
luscious salads, or cold soups, it can also serve as a handsome ice bucket.

Materials

2 large bowls: one 2 inches smaller in diameter than the other
Brightly colored tulips

1. Clear space in your freezer for the larger bowl. Place about 1 inch of water in the bottom and set it in the freezer until the water turns to ice.

2. Set the second bowl inside the first and weigh it down with a brick or heavy can. Push a variety of tulips between the bowls halfway up the side of the inner bowl, then fill to the same height with tepid water. Return to the freezer until the water has frozen.

3. Repeat, adding more tulips and water.

4. To use, pour some hot water into the inner bowl and let it sit for about 8 to 10 minutes or until the bowl can be removed. By this time the outer bowl should also be loose. If it isn't, dip the bowl very quickly into a basin of hot water. Turn the ice bowl out onto a platter.

SWEET TULIPS

For a very special ending to a festive meal, these can be filled with ice cream, berries or whatever you like!

Makes 6 tulip cups

6 organically grown tulips
12 ounces semi-sweet chocolate chips
Pastry brush
6 fresh tulip leaves
Ice cream or berries

1. Gently wash and dry the tulips, then cut off the stems as close to the flower as possible.
2. Melt the chocolate in the microwave or over hot water. Holding the inverted flower by the pistil, use a pastry brush to carefully paint the outside with a generous layer of melted chocolate. Avoid getting chocolate on the inside surfaces to make the tulip easier to remove. Set upsidedown on a bottle to dry. When the chocolate has hardened, gently pull the tulip out. If the petals tear, the pieces can be removed individually, but don't worry if a few shreds remain; remember, tulips are edible. Store in the refrigerator until ready to serve.
3. To serve, make a small lengthwise slit about 2 inches from the bottom of each tulip leaf. Insert the pointed end through the slit, pulling it through to create a small circular stand. Set this on the serving plate. Fill the tulip cup with ice cream or berries and set on the stand.

A BOUQUET OF BOWLS

Since tulips are edible, their flowers make natural bowls in which to serve a variety of foods. (Always use organically grown flowers.) Pinch out the stamens and pistil with your fingernails, gently rinse the flowers in water, then cut off the stem as close to the flower as possible. Make a delicious fruit salad, adding a bit of white wine and sugar, and spoon it into the flowers. Fill them with ice cream or berries and set them in a puddle of raspberry sauce. Offer a platter laden with flowers filled with a variety of salads such as lentil, chicken, tuna, vegetable, or rice. (You may need some lettuce or a few berries to prop up the flowers.)

A TULIP LAMPSHADE

🌷 🌷 🌷 🌷

Materials

White paper lampshade

Loose pages from various size books (antique books have more interesting typography and can be found at yard sales and flea markets)

Color photocopies or laser prints of tulip prints

Adhesive putty from an art supply store

White glue

Paintbrush

Latex polyurethane, matte finish

Burnt umber tint (optional)

1. Pour some glue into a shallow dish and add an equal amount of water. Mix well.
2. Using the paintbrush, apply thinned glue to the back of the first book page and place it on the shade at the top edge, allowing ½ inch at the top of the shade. Fold neatly over the rim to the inside before the glue dries.
3. Continue applying pages one at a time, using differnt sizes and overlapping them randomly in a pleasing pattern. When appropriate, cut pages in half horizontally. Trim the overhang at the top and bottom of the shade to ½ inch and fold over the rim as before.
4. When the entire shade is covered, position the color prints in place with the adhesive.
5. Apply glue to the back of color copies one at a time and affix to the shade.
6. When the glue is completely dry, apply one or two coats of polyurethane to seal and protect the shade. For an antique look, add a touch of burnt umber to the polyurethane.